Hanna's Story
A Tipperary Heritage

by

Anne Loughnane

Grosvenor House
Publishing Limited

All rights reserved
Copyright © Anne Loughnane, 2021

The right of Anne Loughnane to be identified as the author of this work has been asserted in accordance with Section 78 of the Copyright, Designs and Patents Act 1988

The book cover artwork is copyright to Laura Donnelly

This book is published by
Grosvenor House Publishing Ltd
Link House
140 The Broadway, Tolworth, Surrey, KT6 7HT.
www.grosvenorhousepublishing.co.uk

This book is sold subject to the conditions that it shall not, by way of trade or otherwise, be lent, resold, hired out or otherwise circulated without the author's or publisher's prior consent in any form of binding or cover other than that in which it is published and
without a similar condition including this condition being imposed on the subsequent purchaser.

A CIP record for this book
is available from the British Library

ISBN 978-1-83975-805-8

For Jamie, Orna, Maeve and
all my Loughnane nieces and nephews

Sometimes I want to murder time
Sometimes when my heart's aching
But mostly I just stroll along
The path that he is taking

From *October Song*
by the Incredible String Band

Contents

Foreword		ix
Chapter 1	Hanna Meets Pat	1
Chapter 2	A Proposal	6
Chapter 3	Early Married Life	12
Chapter 4	Work on the Farm	18
Chapter 5	Births Proliferate in the shadow of death	24
Chapter 6	Death Strikes again	31
Chapter 7	Looking to her Family's Future	35
Chapter 8	The Family Spreads its Wings	39
Chapter 9	Ireland's Struggle Comes Calling	45
Chapter 10	Personal Anguish Amid the Struggle	48
Chapter 11	A Truce is declared and a Treaty Signed	52
Chapter 12	The Horror of Civil War	60
Chapter 13	A Return to Calmer Waters	64
Epilogue		70
Reading List		72
Acknowledgements		74

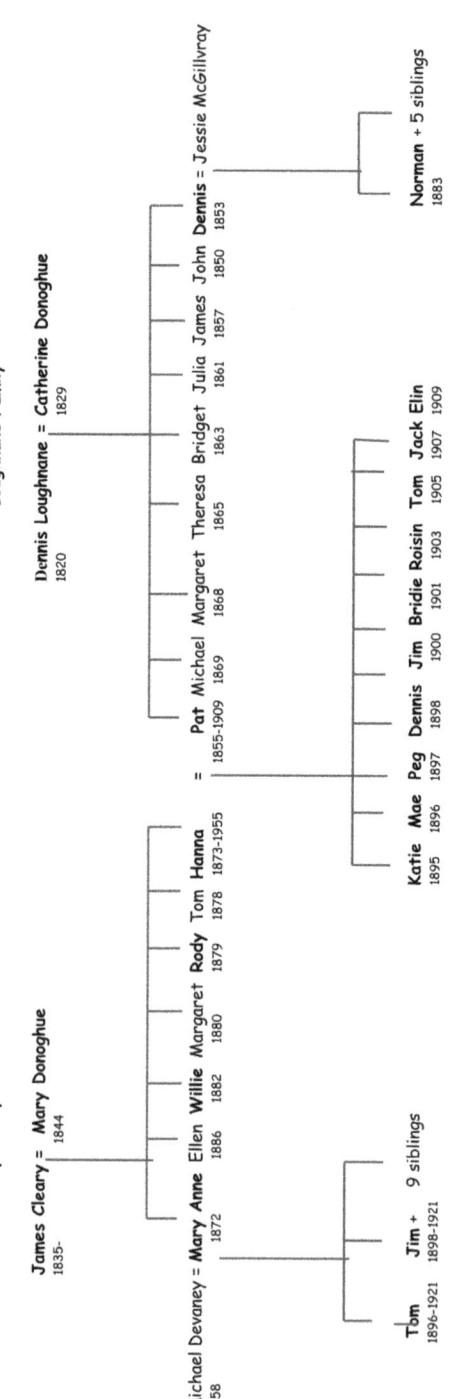

Foreword

My grandmother, Johanna (Hanna) Loughnane, was born Johanna Cleary in 1873. One of seven children, she came from a strong farming family located in Ollatrim, in the parish of Toomevara not far from the market town of Nenagh in North Tipperary. She and her three sisters, Mary Anne, Margaret and Ellen, married substantial local farmers. Her two younger brothers, Rody and Tom, continued to live locally and remained central to her life. Tom inherited the home farm in Ollatrim while Rody, who became one of the first elected Sinn Fein councillors, married into a farm in Knigh, nearer to Nenagh. Her youngest brother Willie, a priest, was initially appointed to serve in a Brooklyn parish in New York. He went on to achieve a brilliant career in the US Army Chaplain Corps, attaining the rank of Brigadier General. He, too, was to play a significant role in her life.

In 1894 Johanna married Patrick (Pat) Loughnane of Reiskmore. Born in 1861, he was one of ten children born to Dennis Loughnane and Catherine Donoghue. Pat inherited the home farm which comprised about a hundred acres of excellent land. It was situated in the townland of Ballymackey and the parish of Toomevara, not far from Johanna's home. Pat had five brothers and four sisters: James, Michael, John, Thomas, Dennis, Margaret, Bridget, Julia and Teresa. James, the eldest, became a priest, and Thomas established a licensed premises in Dublin. Michael and Teresa emigrated to the USA, though Michael subsequently went to Australia where John joined him. The other girls married in Ireland, and the remaining brother, Dennis, joined the British excise service. Dennis was assigned to posts in Scotland and London and was the father of Norman Loughnane who achieved a high rank in the British civil service, and was to have a role in Ireland's transition to independence.

Widowed at thirty five, Johanna was left alone to manage the farm and raise their ten children, the youngest of whom was still in the womb at the time of her husband's death. Her life spanned one of the more turbulent periods of Irish history and her family were closely involved in the fight for independence. I have often wondered how she weathered the difficulties inherent in the responsibilities she carried, compounded by the anxiety associated with the dangers that faced them.

This evocation of her life and times follows their trajectory during those early years of marriage and parenthood. The story is based on historical research (reading list attached) supplemented by an amalgam of archival material such as birth, marriage, death certificates and newspaper coverage as well as memory and information from different members of the family.

In my attempt to bring her story to life, the description of cultural, social and political circumstances as they affected her family are based on real events. The characters of family members and relatives are informed by some familial knowledge and lore, but are largely drawn from imagination, as are the attributions of motivation, personality and the relationship dynamics. The various minor characters introduced are purely fictional. They are, however, set in the real circumstances of time and place which, I hope, renders them credible.

The story's timeline dates from before Hanna's marriage in 1894 to the end of the civil war in 1923. It encompasses the birth of her ten children as follows: Kathleen (Katie), 1895, Mae, 1896, Peg 1897, Dennis, 1898, Jim (my father), 1900, Bridie, 1901, Josephine (Roisin), 1903, Tom, 1905, Jack 1907, and Eilin, 1909. It includes also the deaths of her brother-in-law, Father James Loughnane, just a week before his father Dennis died in January 1897, and her mother-in-law, Catherine, in 1901. There followed the early deaths of her husband and son, Patrick in 1909, and eleven-year old Jack in 1918, as well as those of her young nephews Jim and Tom Devaney in 1921.

> "We shall not leave our children
> Richer store than that deep faith
> Which was her heritage"
>
> Extract from Johanna Loughnane's
> memorial card 1955

CHAPTER 1

Hanna Meets Pat

Hanna wandered out to the farmyard, wiping sudsy hands on her grubby wrap-around overall. There were a number of sheep due to lamb and she worried that they might have moved too near the river. "Joe, try to make sure that the manure is swept into the hollow beside the large cowhouse," her face crinkled in annoyance at the sight of the dung spreading across the cobbled yard. "Yes Ma'am", slow moving solid Joe went to pick up the yard brush leaning against the wall. What would she have done without him all the many years since poor Pat died, "Lord have mercy on his soul", and she smiled at him to take the sting out of her irritability. Tall and dark-haired as a young man, Joe was stooped now, his hair still thick, but grey, though his cheeks and low-browed forehead were surprisingly unlined. He lived alone in his bare little cottage in the lane that led down to the bog. Was he contented with his life? She thought so but didn't really know.

Hanna was proud of her yard surrounded by sturdily built stables, piggery and cowhouses, as well as the large barn and open shelter that housed her trap and sundry farm machinery. The farmyard led into a good-sized haggard where hay and straw were stored in the barns that lay adjacent to a flourishing orchard of apple and plum trees. Here too she kept her fowl, hens, geese, bantams, and a very virile cockerel. Hadn't she been very glad of them and their eggs during the lean years.

Opening the gate into the lane that led to the lower field, she picked her way along the cart ruts, avoiding the dung caused by the funnelling of all the livestock through this narrow passage into the yard. She'd never got round to inserting a little latch gate into a cleaner section of the field. Crows swirled noisily around the old elms and limes as she made her way towards the river which divided the lower from the upper field. She laughed as their caws taunted poor Brandy, her aging sheepdog who barked futilely at the foot of the trees. Relieved to see that the sheep were safely away from the river, she paused a while on the bridge, lazily surveying the amber sheen of the water washing over the pebbles. She felt at peace. She had cared well for the legacy bequeathed to her by Pat when she was just a young woman in her early thirties. His death left her with a family of ten children and a farm to manage. She shuddered now to recall the terrifying years when the family was surrounded by danger barely a decade after his death. Thank God those days were over.

She knew from a cousin that Pat had been a thin schoolboy but wiry and quick at his lessons. The master had liked him and always picked on him to recite or answer multiplication tables when the Inspector came. "That's because he knew he could count on him to perform well," the cousin told her. Though she'd seen him at Mass sometimes, or when he'd come to help them with the harvesting, it was not until she was about sixteen that she could remember ever talking to Pat.

It was at their neighbour Norah Lynch's wake. She had gone with her Mother and sisters Mary Anne and Margaret to pay her respects and had been greeted by Norah's sister Meg. "I'm sorry for your loss Meg," her mother said, shaking hands with her. "Oh, sure she's gone to a better place and didn't she have a grand death, God bless her. Father Tom was with her and gave her the sacrament." A low murmuring of the rosary greeted them in the room where Norah was laid out. It was full of dark shadows and two oil lamps cast pale streams of light over the still corpse. Her hands, intertwined with rosary beads, were crossed mutely over her breast. The clip clop of the horses and the rumble of the traps and sidecars in the yard, formed a backdrop to the quiet murmur of prayer. Hanna remembered noticing the muck on the soles of her mother's shoes as they knelt to join in the prayers. Rising from her knees she had kissed that stone-cold brow before going to join the other neighbours in the kitchen. Here too it was only the light from two large oil lamps and that of the fire and the little lamp burning before the picture of the Sacred Heart that kept the darkness at bay.

She had been glad of the warm fire in the hearth and the lively buzz of conversation and laughter. They weren't sad as, Norah was old at seventy nine, and, as her father said, "had a good innings." The large kettle suspended on a crane over the hearth continually replenished the teapot, and the older women enjoyed this, while she and her sisters drank bottles of lemonade. The men helped themselves to snuff, and the whiskey and porter which were generously available. She noticed Pat talking with his sister, Bride, leaning against the dresser, and for some reason he winked at her, which made her want to giggle. Bride beckoned them over while telling Pat off for his lack of respect. "Begor and what are you talkin about, didn't I have great respect for Norah. Sure she and I were the best of friends!" he said, winking again, which set off more giggles as everyone knew how cantankerous Norah had been. "Just have a bit of respect for the dead," Bride responded turning her back on him to talk to them.

Pat stared in admiration at Mary Anne who was the beauty of the family and drew the eyes of all the young men. Her oval shaped face and hazel eyes were lovely and her glossy mane of chestnut hair was now illumined by bronze highlights under the lamplight. Pat couldn't take his eyes off her.

Mary Anne, however, only had eyes for Michael Devaney, a tall, quiet young man whose unruly hair always seemed in need of a cut. He was a cousin of Pat's and she'd become friendly with him when they both joined a local society founded to promote the Irish language and music. He was passionate about all things Irish and a strong supporter of the Irish Parliamentary Party's fight for Home Rule. Like many of his like-minded friends he had admired Charles Stuart Parnell and been profoundly shocked at the revelations about Parnell's affair with a married woman, for he was a young man with strong religious beliefs about the sanctity of marriage. "Even worse," he told Mary Anne, "was the blow this dealt to their hopes for Home Rule because of the split it's caused in the Party." Michael, like his father before him had been very active in the Tenant's Rights campaign and the Land League that replaced it. He was totally committed to the land movement, as indeed were Pat and his father. She could hear him now arguing vehemently with a neighbour who had come over to join them. As always, they got stuck into politics. "How can you side with that layabout trouble-maker Jimmy Connolly?" Joe asked. "All he's lookin for is a fight and he doesn't care who gets hurt."

"This isn't about what I think of Jimmy Connolly, it's about gettin justice for Irish farmers. Your own father was very glad when we secured the land act of 1881 giving us fair rent, fixity of tenure and the right of a free sale. At least this will compensate us to some extent for our hard work on the farms."

"Well isn't that enough? Why are we carryin on with all this agitation?"

"Because," said Pat, "we should by rights own the land that we and our forefathers have worked. Our hard labour should not be putting money into the hands of landlords who have rarely done a day's work and only come over to lord it over us for the odd week, they and their friends galloping over our land without a by-your-leave and they couldn't care less about the damage to our crops or livestock."

Hanna and Mary Anne, bored by the perennial arguments, went to join some other friends and were soon into plans about what they'd wear at the dance to be held at Slattery's farm in a couple of week's time.

Hanna, though, would later give thanks for the courage and commitment of those young men and their fathers before them. The land legislation they agitated for, and secured, meant that some years later they were enabled to take ownership of land they could previously only hope to tenant. The day that Colonel Bowen of Bowen's Court sold the deeds of Reiskmore to Pat's father was the only occasion that she'd seen that old man cry.

CHAPTER 2

A Proposal

Indeed it was not that dance that she could recall now, but one that took place a couple of years later at Mrs Moriarty's on the occasion of her son Kevin's departure for America. Change was afoot in Hanna's family during those years and it was the "drawing home of the turf" that started it all off. Her father had turf cutting rights in the local bog and the turf had already been cut and stacked earlier in the summer. This was hard, hard work and a job they all hated but usually it was her two brothers, Tom and Rody, who helped their father with this. "Harness up the ass and cart Margaret and let you and Ellie go and fetch the turf home," her father said one fine day in early September. Margaret wasn't pleased and muttered to her mother. "Everyone will see me Mam and I'll be shamed, none of the other girls have to do this." "Hush now," said her mother sternly, "and go and do as your father asks you." Normally good humoured and merry, Margaret set off in a bad mood.

While not beautiful like Mary Anne, she was a handsome girl and her normally cheery personality made her popular with everyone. Her sister Ellie, a sunny little girl, was great friends with Margaret and could usually pull her out of the sulks. But not that day! Joe Maher and his friend Pat Harty had arrived to bring their turf home at the same time. "Nice to see other folk doing a hand's turn," said Joe and got a smile from Ellie. Margaret carried on scowling while shifting the sods onto the cart. The footings (little heaps of turf) were all dried out and ready to load, and when finished they threw a bag of old hay on top of the turf to cushion them for the ride back.

Half-way down the lane that led to the bog they could hear a rumble from the right-hand cartwheel. Alarmed, they hopped off and sure enough, they could see that the axle was cracked. Joe and Pat arrived not long after and came to see what could be done.

"Margaret, let you run down to O'Brien's cottage," Pat said, "and see if they have a bit of old rope. Ellie, you and I may as well go on ahead and Joe here can see Margaret and the turf safely home, it's not too far out of his way."

In fact, he had to borrow a cart from the O'Briens and transfer all the turf on to it, but astonishingly Margaret arrived home in great good humour. Ellie was then only a child of six or seven and this was the first time she met the man she would one day marry.

It was not long after this, that Hanna and her sisters walked up the short drive to the Moriarty's house on a bright autumnal day to help with the preparations for the dance. For some reason she could still recall the delicate tracery of the bare willow branches by the stream that ran along that side of the house. They were beautiful that afternoon, burnished to a luminous copper by the late afternoon sun. The three sisters had set out together and she recalled their excitement at the thought of the evening ahead. "Pat says he'll give us a lift home in the sidecar," Margaret told them.

"Sure it's a grand night, I might walk", Mary Anne replied. They'd all smiled as Margaret retorted. "Sure of course you will Mary Anne. Won't it be Michael Devaney that will be keeping you company!" Mary Anne blushed but said nothing.

Young Tadg Moriarty was rolling the second of two barrels of porter, bought in for the occasion, through the back door as they approached the house. Pat arrived just behind them with his fiddle accompanied by their farmhand, Joe, with his concertina. He and Pat had grown up together and they were both mad for music and dancing. There was a strong bond between them for all the difference in their stations.

Moriarty's kitchen was festive with a bright fire in the hearth. There were a good number of oil lamps casting a cheery glow over the furniture with the pictures of Robert Emmet and Parnell looking down on them. The big kitchen table was pushed back against the wall to make room for the dancing and there were mounds of sandwiches and cakes covered with a clean tablecloth for later.

Pat had been quiet that evening as it had become generally known that Michael Devaney was now openly courting Mary Anne and that they had an understanding which put an end to his own hopes. Liking him, Hanna was a bit sad about this but was glad to see him cheering up as the music and dancing took hold, and everyone admired the lively agility with which he and Joe created such a merry party for them all. She had heard that he could dance on a sixpence and laughed out loud when later in the evening he treated them to a performance which made no lie of the rumour. Like many of the other young men he'd had a fair amount of porter drunk by then but still never missed a beat. Hanna herself had a sweet voice and when asked for a song, it was Tom Moore's lovely melody, *Sweet Vale of Avoca*, that she sang. She could still remember Pat's eyes on her as she finished:

HANNA'S STORY: A TIPPERARY HERITAGE

*Where the storms that we feel in this cold world should cease
And our hearts like thy waters be mingled in peace*

She had blushed then. However it was Kevin Moriarty's wonderfully comical song, sent to him by his brother in Philadelphia that had been the musical highlight of the evening:

*Have you seen me Uncle Dan McCann..
A typical bit of a Galway man
He came out to the USA in the year of '61*

With Mary Anne's future more or less settled, Hanna and Margaret spent long evenings discussing the way ahead for them. It was a visit by a cousin who worked in a hospital in Dublin which set their sights on nursing as a career. They were both excited at the thought of going to Dublin to do their training. Then came the invitation to a dance in Reiskmore, Pat's home. It was her first visit and she liked the simple solidity of the two-storied farmhouse. The glowing burgundy of the Virginian creeper that covered the front of the house was beautiful under the evening light, and the narrow flower-bed running the length of the front facade was still offering some autumnal colour from late flowering roses. The gravel frontage to the house ended in a hedged oval, from the centre of which grew a magnificent chestnut tree with its base encircled by a white painted seat. Attractive fencing, also painted white, separated the house from a well mown lawn in front, which, Pat told her, "did for a tennis court in summer".

It was an evening that was to change the future envisaged by both herself and Margaret. She had only a vague memory of the music and fun, though she recalled noting with some surprise that Margaret was whirled around energetically by Jim Gilmartin in a "Siege of Ennis" and again in the "Walls of

Limerick." He was a large kindly farmer with a great sense of humour and that night he and Margaret made a very merry couple. At the end of the evening Jim offered to drive herself and Margaret home and Pat said he needed some fresh air and would come along for the ride. He lit the way out to the haggard, his lantern softening the blackness of the night, where Jim harnessed the pony and sidecar. She jumped with fright when the shriek of a night owl pierced the stillness and was glad of the stirrings of the beasts in the nearby outhouses. As the thud of the pony's hooves established their hypnotic rhythm Pat said, "give us an 'oul song Hanna," and it was that rhythmic child's song that she sang:

Óró 'Sé do bheatha 'bhaile
Óró 'Sé do bheatha 'bhaile

It seemed to chime with the trotting hooves. When she finished Pat said, "did you know that was a song meant to accompany the hauling home of a bride to her new home by her husband?" She had blushed, confused by the question.

About a month later, having been to the house to ask for her father's blessing, Pat surprised her in the orchard picking windfalls. He asked her to sit down and said abruptly "I'd like us to get married Hanna." She had an inkling for some time that he liked her, yet she retorted equally abruptly, "weren't you mad about Mary Anne?"

"I was," he replied, "she's a beautiful girl and I think all the boys were in love with her, but that's in the past now and I think she'll be very happy with Michael. You and I suit Hanna, and I'll have no regrets if you agree to be my wife."

"I don't know if I want to marry Pat, the boys say that we'd be just like the animals! Maybe I should be a nun."

"We can just be great friends like St Francis and St Clare," Pat said.

She laughed: "They didn't sleep together."

"How do you know" he'd retorted.

"Why do you want to marry anyway?"

"I'm lonely" he said.

"Indeed and you're not, don't you have your parents."

"But they'll die and what would I do then."

"Can't you live with one of your sisters"?

"I could, I suppose, but I'd far rather live with you Hanna."

Well, he'd taken hold of her hand by then and she found that she didn't want to refuse him. She wasn't yet twenty and he was thirty two. In spite of the troubles ahead, she'd never have any regrets.

CHAPTER 3

EARLY MARRIED LIFE

Hanna was married on Shrove Tuesday and it was a wild wet day in early March. She had to hold on to her lovely little hat which would otherwise have been blown away by the wind. She saw that the remaining daffodils and late crocuses were already flattened as they made an undignified run for the coach. Pat, looking uncharacteristically groomed, waited for her at the Church. The ceremony and wedding breakfast passed in a haze of good-humoured chat and congratulations before they found themselves on a train bound for Lahinch, where they spent their honeymoon.

"What's wrong with your dinner? You've hardly eaten a pick."

"I'm not hungry," she said, staring at him in astonishment. How could he eat so heartily. Had he no feelings? "I think I might have a fever coming," she added agitatedly.

He looked at her shrewdly. "Yes, I can see that, I think maybe we should be quiet and just sleep tonight."

She'd felt less anxious then but recalled the curiously hollow feeling of disappointment. Pat was a wonderful storyteller and he set himself to entertain her, so that by the time they went up to their bedroom she was laughing so much that she'd forgotten her fever and fright. Her anxiety had started to return when he said;

"Now Hanna," we've all the time in the world to get used to each other and I don't want to hurt you, so if you need to, you can tell me stop any time you want to," and he looked on her with such tender affection that she found it easy to give herself to him.

Their days in Lahinch passed in a daze of fun and laughter. It was a bright early spring day when they took a coach trip to the cliffs of Moher. She loved the way the majesty of the cliffs was gradually revealed to them as the little winding road wound its way through an expansive landscape. They crept to the very edge of the headland and lay flat, gazing down that vertical drop and watching the sea birds as they swirled fearlessly over the ferocious waves lashing the cliffs below. They had their picnic, well set back from this awesome ledge, listening to the cries of the gulls and curlews.

There had been the fun of the afternoon spent at a fair overlooking the beach, with stalls selling all kinds of sweets, cheap jewellery, rosary beads and even dillisk (sea-weed) which she'd tasted and spat out. Pat ate some and said that it was very good for you. They watched the jugglers and brass bands and she had her fortune told by a gypsy woman with a tartan shawl and dirty fingernails who scared her a little with her black eyes and harshly lined face. Pat put his foot down when she suggested a third go on the chairoplanes:

"I'm sick as a dog Hanna and I'm not putting another foot inside a chairoplane"

She'd laughed and they wandered around listening to the ballad singers, many of them tinkers. She was surprised by the respect with which Pat listened to them.

"We owe a debt to these folk who have carried and cherished our culture Hanna."

Truth to tell she hadn't thought that there was much to cherish after listening to a third raucous rendition of *The Rising of the Moon* by yet another, down-at-heel balladeer. They were on their way out of the fair when Pat pulled her to a standstill in front of a little wizened man. A small group of people had already gathered to listen. She was surprised when the singer ignored the applause at the end of the song and didn't thank those who threw money into his cap. He hitched up his worn trousers, kept in place with a bit of old rope, and began to sing a lament about the downfall of the noble house of Butler in Tipperary, *Cill Chais,* and the laying waste of the woodland around it:

> *Now what will we do for timber*
> *With the last of the woods laid low?*
> *There's no talk of Cill Chais or its household*
> *And its bell will be struck no more*

They had been silenced by the lyrical passion with which he delivered this poignant lament. His voice was roughened and frail, but still musical. Pat dropped a whole florin into his cap.

"He's worth a lot more than that Hanna," he said curtly when she commented on his generosity.

Over at last, they headed for home, the home of her parents-in-law. She was apprehensive. His father Dennis was a confident, jovial man of whom she was a little in awe, but she knew Kitty to be a kindly woman and this was a comfort. It was she who told her to call them Mother and Father and indeed that was how she always thought of them. It had been a long journey and they were cheered by the warmth of the wood fire that greeted them on arrival. Her initial shyness was banished by the heated argument in progress between Father and his friend Matt Delaney.

"We'll never get Home Rule unless we take matters into our own hands," Father was asserting vehemently. "Sure, that was the only reason why we made such progress on the land front. If it hadn't been for Parnell and his boycotting strategies, rent strikes and the like, we'd have got nowhere, God rest his soul. I don't know when we'll see his like again."

"Sure weren't we hoodwinked into thinking him a respectable man," retorted Matt, "and him carrying on all the time with a married woman."

"And I suppose that made him a poor leader," said Father sarcastically. "If it hadn't been for him, Matt Delaney, neither you nor I would be sitting securely on our land now. He is the reason why we're no longer fearful of rack rents or of being thrown out onto the side of the road, and wasn't our nation of mealymouthed hypocrites quick to forget what they owed to him?"

Mother smiled, throwing her eyes up to Heaven, "Pay no attention to them child, they just like arguing." She had relaxed then, watching the sparks of cheery light thrown out by the logs and the rosy glow of the oil lamps reflected in the sideboard mirror.

Indeed she was used to a vibrant political atmosphere though she paid little attention to their detailed arguments in those days. Her own brothers were ardent nationalists, and forever talking politics. She knew that both families had secured ownership of their land as a result of the land agitation that led to the Ashbourne Act in 1885, then the Wyndham act of 1903 offering attractive repayment conditions. She did, over time, come to appreciate the very different political stances reflected in the heated debates that raged around her. Father, and indeed Pat, had some sympathy for the old Fenian advocacy of armed struggle in order to achieve independence while the bulk of their neighbours supported the Irish Parliamentary Party's non-violent constitutional route to reform. She'd been very surprised to learn that though the church was mostly opposed to their tactics, some priests and indeed Bishop Fogarty of Killaloe, a cousin of Mother's, would later support their more republican sympathies.

It was Mother who was to exert a more abiding influence on her life and spirit. She was a profoundly religious woman whose faith was nourished by a life of daily personal prayer supplemented by the family rosary each night and rigorous adherence to the requirements of the Church's liturgical round. This was the sure anchor around which family life orbited, and, young as she was, Hanna gradually absorbed responsibility for ensuring its continuance. "You know, if the stones of this house could talk," an elderly neighbour said to her one day, "they'd surely pray."

Mother's serenity and warmth had sheltered her immaturity and protected her from many of the pitfalls of early married life. It was she who ensured that they had their share of fun amid the rigorous round of farm life. She would shoo them out to local dances and parties when work was finished for the day. She'd also insist that they took the day off to attend events such as the annual agricultural show and the point-to-point in Nenagh. Hanna recalled some of Father's grumbles. "Sure isn't their whole life a holiday, how am I going to fence the lower field on my own."

"And isn't there tomorrow," Mother would retort and they'd gleefully set off.

Most memorable, however, were the nights when they'd slip off to bed, Pat proclaiming a tiredness that deceived no one and she, blushingly, glad to go with him. They had to pass through his parent's bedroom to the inner one they shared, grateful for the thick walls that gave them a bit of privacy. She was astonished by the pleasure and excitement their bodies' closeness afforded and sometimes a little ashamed. When she mentioned something of this to her once, Mother replied, "sure isn't it a blessing child that the Good Lord made it so easy for us to conceive more of his children. You'll make up for it later with the trouble they bring!"

The annual round of farming life gradually absorbed Hanna. Perhaps it was knowing that the farm would belong to Pat and herself one day that gave such a zest to her growing interest in it.

CHAPTER 4

Work on the Farm

Hanna's memories of those early years on the farm were vivid.

"You'll need to take the milk to the creamery this morning Hanna," Pat said. "I'll harness the pony and cart for you. Joe needs help to round up the bullocks for the fair tomorrow."

She was excited, never having been to the creamery before. Mother explained to her how they used to have to separate the cream by laying the milk out in pans, and waiting for the cream to come to the top before churning it by hand, to make the butter. They would pack it into firkins and sell it to the butter merchant in Nenagh. "We have it easy now because some clever man in Sweden invented the mechanical separator and we have creameries all over the country using the new machinery."

"What we need", Father piped up, "are co-operative creameries run by ourselves, like that chap Horace Plunkett of the IAOS (Irish Agricultural Organisation Society) recommends. The private companies who own most of them only care about their profits. Why don't you and some of the other young farmers around get together?" He said to Pat.

"Sure, aren't we all right as we are?" Pat retorted. He was more of a dreamer than his energetic father whom he often exasperated. They still made their own butter for the family, she and Mother taking it in turns to rotate the big barrel churn with a crank handle.

Arriving in Toomevara she squealed with delight. "Mary Anne, Mary Anne," she burst out laughing, for there was her elegant sister trying to back an ass and cart carrying large milk cans toward the landing area. The donkey was clearly not in the mood to cooperate! "Oh Hanna," Mary Anne wailed. "I can't get her to do anything. Our pony has pulled a leg muscle, I have to rely on this amadan."

Two neighbouring men watching the donkey's antics with some amusement strolled over, "Well bejabbers, Ma'am, I don't think you'll get any good of her," one of them told her flustered sister as they helped her lift the cans into the creamery.

"I'm never going to drive this imbecile of an animal again," Mary Anne said when she thanked them. It had been great to meet up with her sisters during those early years when their lives were all expanding.

"Hanna, can you take the eggs into Nenagh to sell," Mother would often suggest, knowing how much she enjoyed the outings when she would arrange to meet up with her sisters or cousins. Though the work of the farm gave little time for social life, she loved to visit the family and enjoyed meeting friends at weddings and church services, as well as the odd dance.

"Let ye keep a close eye on the ewes tonight," Father said. "The Howards over by Woodville had four killed last night by a stray dog." It was lambing time and her favourite time of the year. The late nights, when she and Pat did a final check of the ewes before bed-time, were often beautiful; sometimes the star filled or moonlit skies stilled them with awe but, just as often, with hats pulled down against the rain, they hurried through the muck-filled entrance to a nearby paddock where they had gathered the ewes in for ease of supervision. Here the sheepcock, a low cock of hay built around a central pole, ensured that food was always available to them. This made it easy to deal with any trouble during the lambing season.

They would be out again not long after five in the morning to check that all was well. She revelled in those early spring mornings, the grass sparkling with dew and little blue anemones and buttercups peeping through the grass. The emerging whitethorn blossom and fresh fuzz of new green on the bushes and trees made a fitting backdrop to the drama of birth and occasionally death. She had loved rearing the orphaned or rejected lambs each year and always kept them near her in the yard. Many's the time she took a fall as they rushed affectionately (or hungrily!) to greet her, oblivious to their growing strength.

"That's it Hanna, out they go to the paddock," Pat said after yet another tumble. "You think they're still lambs but they're almost grown sheep now." They did butt her mercilessly but she hated to see them go.

Raising sheep created a lot of work. She was very glad she wasn't called upon to help with the sheep dipping, which happened two or three times a year to protect the sheep from the biting fly. This was heavy work when the sheep had to be caught by their four legs and lobbed on their backs into the tank of dip. The poor frightened creatures would suffer this two or three times before they were released.

In early May when the sheep were due to be shorn, Pat would say, "Help us set up the pen in the orchard Hanna." It was her job to get the fire lit for the tar pot which was used to brand the shorn animals with Pat's initials. The fleece of each sheep was spread out on the wooden deck of the hay tram with the tails hanging over the end ledge for trimming. "Be very careful to only cut off the dirty bits because we get paid by weight and we don't want to lose any good fleece" Pat warned.

Hanna recalled the one time she had to assist when they killed the pig. Normally a couple of neighbours helped Father and Pat but they were short of a man on that day. Mother spent the morning boiling up a huge cauldron of water in readiness. "Hanna you'll have to give us a hand, we need a fourth person to hang onto the pig's ear," Pat said.

The low heavy table on its four sturdy blocky legs was already in the yard near to the pig sty. This was called a "sheep" for some strange reason. Father, encased in an apron made from washed flour bags, stood at its head. He had a sharp pointed spike around half a foot in length with an iron handle attached to the middle of the spike. "Let you take hold of the other ear Hanna," Pat said, having grabbed one ear himself. Joe grasped the pig's tail in one hand holding a heavy mallet in the other.

"Pull it onto the table," Father instructed, but so terrible were the poor pig's screams that Hanna let go of the ear in fright. "For God's sake woman will you keep a hold of it," Father thundered.

"Hush Dennis, sure isn't it the child's first time having to do this."

Mother placed her hand over hers and thankfully they got the poor beast on to the table at her second try. Father then centred the pointed spike on the pig's forehead and Joe struck a heavy blow of the mallet. The pig fell to the ground unconscious and the men lifted it onto the table on its back where Father stabbed it in the heart with a very sharp knife.

Hanna turned and ran into a nearby stable where she was violently sick.

"Let you go to her Pat, poor child," Mother said. She had to keep stirring the blood flowing from the pig into the clean bucket to cool it. Still feeling shaky, she returned with her to the house. She saw the men washing the pig's intestines at the pump, having turned them inside out before scraping them thoroughly. "We'll be able to use them for black and white puddings," Mother told her. More boiling water was poured over the pig before the men scraped all the hair and any blemishes off the body. It was then hung in the barn wrapped in a clean cloth until the following day when it was carved up into sizeable chunks and salted with special cheap curing salt. Pieces of pork were shared out among family and neighbours.

She helped Mother layer and salt the new bacon in a clean wooden tub. The head was sawn in two so that it could fit into the pot. She could never face eating this, though Father held it to be the tastiest part of the pig. Mother taught her how to make the black and white pudding that they all loved. "You simmer the blood for over half an hour, then mix in finely chopped onion, milk, breadcrumbs, spices and some chopped lard," she told her "and for the white pudding add in some pork from around the kidney area of the pig."

Toward late summer they all kept an anxious eye on the weather, praying for the sunny spell needed to cut and save the hay without damage. She smiled now at how rose tinged her memories were. They can't have all been golden sun-drenched days. She recalled the sound of swishing scythes as the bronzed grasses gave way to their fate. How she loved to carry baskets filled with ham sandwiches and thickly buttered barn brack to the fields at mid-day, and to watch the men and the children devour them with gusto. The younger children would spend the day playing hide and seek amongst the growing hay ricks, waiting for the highlight of their day, the ride home to the farm atop the ricks. These were loaded onto the slanting hay trams and brought back to the haggard where the hay was forked up into the big barn.

There was always great excitement at the corn threshing when the old steam thresher appeared in the haggard and a number of the neighbours came to help. This had been wonderful fun when she and Pat were first married and the day would often end with an impromptu dance in the evening. As their young family rapidly grew, however, it became a lot more exhausting. "Be sure and keep the children out of the way, I don't want them running under the feet of the men," Pat would warn. This was easier said than done when she was run off her feet with so much food to be prepared and cooked.

These had been good years: she was glad of the comforting memories and, indeed, that she didn't know then what lay ahead of her.

CHAPTER 5

BIRTHS IN THE SHADOW OF DEATH

Despite growing up on a farm and being used to animals giving birth, Hanna had been extraordinarily ignorant of the details of pregnancy and birth. It was Mary Anne, the first of her sisters to have a family, who enlightened her. She was appalled when she learnt that babies did not emerge through the belly button, and "Oh the shame... how could you possibly let the doctor, a man, examine you down there?" None of this seemed to matter when Mother said, a year or so after they were married, "I think you must be in the family way Hanna, I'll let out a couple of your skirts and maybe make a nice pinafore dress, we could use that pretty material with the daisy pattern." Clearly pleased, she had given her a quick hug.

Having been nauseous most mornings for a month, Hanna was pretty sure that she was pregnant but had not liked to say anything to Pat as she knew that miscarriages were common with a first pregnancy. She told him that night and he seemed strangely shocked. "Surely you must have been expecting it Pat?" "Of course, of course, I know it's daft but it never seemed real. Are you all right, will you be all right?" She made reassuring noises, feeling suddenly a lot older than him. She had a premonition then that it was she who would need to be the calm and steady presence in the family, and indeed the years ahead would prove this was the case.

"Oh, I do hope it won't be too hard on the child," she overheard Mother say one night as her time approached. "Sure, she'll be fine, isn't she young and healthy?" Father replied. "And I suppose you'd know that with all your experience," Mother retorted drily. "'Tis little men know of the suffering of women."

In the event Hanna endured seven long hours of labour while Mother and Brigid the local midwife held her hand and wiped the perspiration from her face, making encouraging and soothing noises. "Mother Mary help...Jesus, Mary and Joseph help me," she'd whispered between screams of agony as the waves of searing pain struck again and again. Pat was distraught, and came to the door repeatedly, his own face white as a sheet, but was urged away by his mother and Brigid. Eventually little Kathleen emerged, "Oh, she's perfect love," Mother was crying and Hanna had smiled through her exhaustion as the little creature was placed in her arms. "I'm never going through that again," she whispered to Pat as he held his baby daughter. "Lord no Hanna, never again love," he replied fervently, tears of relief pouring down his face.

Hanna had frequent cause to reflect on these less than prophetic words over the years as pregnancies and births followed in quick succession. Pat was, at times, stricken with remorse, "I know I'm wearing you out Hanna," and would try to restrain himself from, as he said, "bothering her." Sure he wasn't entirely to blame, they were young and their bodies yearned towards each other during those early years of marriage.

It was when she was pregnant with Peg, her third child, that Pat's brother James died. He was a parish priest in Newmarket-on-Fergus and only forty seven years of age. Mother and

Father were in shock and could hardly bear to leave his graveside after the burial. It must have been there on that cold morning that Father caught the pneumonia which killed him just a week later.

Father had been struggling to breathe all through the night as Mother sat by his side praying repeated decades of the rosary and wiping saliva that dribbled down his chin. It was when Pat took her place, insisting that she try to get some rest, that he passed away. "I was glad she wasn't there," he told Hanna. "The old man seemed agitated and gave a horrible croaking sound before dying and at least she didn't see that." Hanna was awed by the courage with which Mother attended his Requiem Mass and funeral, barely a week after burying her son. Pat held her arm as they stumbled over the uneven ground that led to the family plot in the lea of an old ruined Church in Ballygibbon graveyard. She recalled marvelling at the beauty of the frosted bushes and trees that sparkled under a cold wintry sun, smiling heartlessly down on so much pain.

Father's death was not a great loss for Hanna. His life had centred around the demands of farming and his absorption in political matters, such as Home Rule and the Land Courts, did not interest her then. Unlike herself and Pat, who loved a bit of music and dancing on social occasions, Father liked nothing better than a game of cards. Far bleaker for her had been the gradual loss of Mother who seemed to shrink into herself after her husband's death. Always of a profound faith, she became consumed by religious matters, reciting endless novenas and decades of the rosary. All Pat's efforts to chivvy an interest in life were to no avail and gradually, she lost interest even in the children in whom she had delighted.

For Hanna it was a lonely time. Mother had been her companion during those early years of marriage and she sorely missed her. It was nearly two years after Father's death when their fourth child and first son was born, and it was his birth that briefly restored Mother to the family. "He's brought his grandfather back to us Hanna," she would say repeatedly and had been delighted when they christened him Dennis. She doted on the child and paid no attention when Hanna told her that he was "in a fair way to being totally ruined."

Hanna did not let on to Mother that this first-born son of hers had awakened a strange and baffling tenderness in her too. She was not a sentimental woman but had a practical caring love for all her children. Dennis was different: "Perhaps," she thought, "it's because he's a boy." She was quite sure that he was not going to be like his grandfather and, though she didn't tell Mother so, felt in her bones that he would be more like Pat. Her love for this child was tinged with an anxiety that never left her, but she would not have been without the joy that his endearing nature also brought to her. It was a relief that no such anxiety had accompanied the arrival of her second son, Jim, two years later.

Barely a year after Jim's birth she found herself pregnant yet again. She was just twenty seven and she had five children under the age of six. She felt despairing. "I don't want any more children, I'm worn out," she'd raged at Pat, "but little you care except for your own pleasure."

"Hush Hanna, you are just tired, sure what can we do if it's God's will and aren't all our children fine and healthy."

"And isn't it convenient to put the blame for your own selfish urges at God's door."

"The children are stirring, they'll need their breakfast," he said, trying to deflect her anger.

"Well let you feed them then," she said, and turning had sobbed into her pillow. He'd looked at her helplessly.

Mother was stirring in the next room and would have overheard but she didn't care, nor had she cared for Pat's shamed embarrassment. When they discussed it he would willingly agree that they should try and refrain from having more children, but in the moment It seemed impossible for him to practice restraint. And she too found it hard to say no with their young bodies in such close proximity. However it seemed to her an increasingly high price to pay in fatigue and pain for such momentary pleasure.

She stayed in bed all that morning and when she came downstairs Mother, bless her. had lit the fire in the dining room and insisted that she put her feet up, while she made a cup of tea. The kindness of the old lady, herself in poor health, had set the tears rolling again and she tried to apologise. "Hush, pet, sure you're worn out and I know it's hard. All we can do is offer up our sufferings to our Blessed Lord and pray to his Holy Mother to intercede for the faith and courage to endure."

She was to regret the extent to which she had let the coolness that followed her row with Pat harden into a definite distancing, primarily because of the distress it caused Mother. Her health and energy declined swiftly after Jim's birth in February 1900 and she retreated more and more into a life of prayer taking little interest in the day to day life of the family or farm. She slipped inexorably away from them, though reviving unexpectedly one day in August, when she thought that she could sit out in the sun for a while. It was not to be. The following morning Pat found her dead in her bed. "She's gone," he said, tears streaming down his face.

Hanna didn't cry then but she was surely bereft. Mother had been closer to her than her own mother and when she looked at her dead face so peaceful and strangely young, now gone forever, she felt lonelier than she'd ever felt in her life. Apart from her kindly support and practical help Mother understood the weight of care on her young shoulders and did all she could to ease her burden. Oh how she would miss her. They buried her beside Father in the family plot on a day when sunshine and showers followed each other, speckling the mourners with droplets of light.

Pat and herself made up their differences after the death of his mother, their shared grief bringing a return of a measure of warmth. He did try during subsequent years to practice restraint and thankfully larger gaps intervened between the pregnancies that followed. However, the light-hearted unity of their early years was gone, replaced by a practical friendly relationship where each understood and accepted their respective roles. Absorbed as she was in the care of her growing family, she had known that Pat felt the loss of their earlier closeness more than she did. In those days he would always invite her to go with him to attend a dance or supper with a neighbour or member of the family. She recalled one of his many urgings: "Let you come with me to Moroney's Hanna, 'twill be a grand night and we'll get Annie (their housemaid) to stay with the children." But as usual, she declined, being too tired or concerned with one or other of the children.

So it was that increasingly, he would go out on his own, often taking his fiddle as he was always in great demand for social gatherings. On quieter evenings there would be a friend to meet in the pub, ostensibly about some matter to do with the farm when he would often arrive home having had a quantity to drink. She did worry about this but when she tried to talk to him he brushed it aside. "Can't a man have a sociable pint with a friend without being nagged at."

She sometimes felt guilty of neglecting him, as, while caring for her growing brood of little ones satisfied her, she knew that

Pat often found them noisy and tiresome and was glad to seek out the company of friends and neighbours. She was resigned to the fact that his way of dealing with worry and responsibility was to rely a little too much on drink and conviviality. Nevertheless his decency, kindly nature and delight in music brought a lot of fun to their lives.

In the eight years before his death in 1909 Hanna gave birth to three more children, two little boys, Jack and Tom, and a little girl baptised Josephine but always known as Roisin. She was carrying their youngest child Eilin, when Pat died. By then her uncle William had also died unexpectedly in Dublin. it was to be a decade haunted by cruel deaths.

CHAPTER 6

DEATH STRIKES AGAIN

Hanna heard him tiptoeing down the narrow stairs in his stockinged feet that morning. It was almost entirely dark except for a faint light coming through the small bedroom window. Though she fixed up his ham sandwiches the night before, she had, unusually for her, risen to see him off. The acrid smell of the turf filled the kitchen, and she was touched by his thoughtfulness in getting it lit before he left. She could hear the thud of his boots on the cobbled yard where he'd no doubt been feeding the beasts. Shuffling into a pair of his old boots she went to join him. "You're looking forward to your day's shooting," she said.

"I am that, and we'll have a grand day of it."

They leant together on the gates overlooking their misty fields, the elms and beeches still releasing heavy droplets of rain for it had been a wet night. The tip of his cigarette gleamed brightly in the half light and he topped it quickly between his fingers at the approach of Mike Flaherty's pony and car. Pat went to fetch his gun and shooting bag and was gone with a quick wave.

Hanna was dismayed to see a bitter wind developing later in the morning, driving relentless sleet and rain: surely they would give up and come home. It was, however, late afternoon by the time Pat returned. He was wet to the bone and though warmed by the fire and a change of clothes, he became shivery later that evening. "You'll need to go to bed Pat and I'm very much afraid that you've caught a bad cold."

She made him a hot lemon drink with cloves and he was indeed relieved to go to bed. His laboured breathing and feverish moans woke her in the early hours and, seriously alarmed, she shook Dennis awake. "Let you harness the pony and ride down to the Flaherty's and ask Mrs Flaherty to come quickly, your father is ill." Sensing the urgency the boy ran to do her bidding and soon Nellie Flaherty arrived. She'd pressed Hanna's hand in sympathy but wasted no time in chat. Together they changed the bed which was soaking and spent the next two days trying to make him comfortable and bring his temperature down with cold compresses. By the second day when there was no improvement they sent for the doctor.

"He's very weak Hanna," Doctor Courtney was gentle, "but you're doing all the right things." He must have contacted Father Hogan their local parish priest, as he arrived shortly afterwards and gave Pat Extreme Unction. He had probably known that there was no hope.

Pat died that night. Hanna sat beside him praying the whole time and must have dozed off slightly when his death rattle jerked her awake. She continued to sit there until Nellie, who had stayed to look after the family, came into the room in the morning. Hanna could recall her closing his eyes gently and putting her arms around her. It was Nellie who laid him out and contacted her family. They made arrangements for the funeral and Mary Anne and Ellie came to stay with her, week about, to care for the children.

The image of that darkened candle-lit room with the picture of Our Lady of Perpetual Succour looking down on the still corpse of her husband, would haunt the years ahead. Hanna had no recollection of the wake or the funeral and burial or even the weeks following his death. She supposed that she must have cared for the children and carried out the normal chores and knew that it was her brother Tom, who rode over from his farm some four or five miles away each day, who saw to the needs of the livestock and farm. Tom became her main support in managing the farm over the years ahead. It was only when her little fatherless girl was born, the child she was carrying when Pat died, that the tears came and seemed to keep coming.

She knew that she was distressing the children as her tearful sadness overwhelmed her repeatedly, but she couldn't help it.

"I'll look after you Mam, you don't need to cry," she recalled Dennis' anxious attempts to make her happy. "I'll take you out for a jaunt in the trap, I can harness it and all."

Dazed and forlorn, she managed to feed little Eilin but seemed unable to do much else. It was her eldest girls, with the help of Annie their domestic help, who took over the care of the little ones during the weeks that followed and, though looking back she regretted the abrupt end to their childhood, she could not have managed without their help. "Let you get them dressed Katie, and you light the fire Annie, I'll get the porridge on," she would hear Mae, who had always been a good organiser, issue instructions. Katie, the eldest, was a gentle and caring soul who cushioned the little ones from the impact of her grief.

Peg was more of a tomboy who loved to read and hoped for an adventurous life. She had been a bit of a pet of Pat's and had felt his death even more keenly than the others. Nevertheless, together with her sisters she carried out these and other chores without demur. The animals had to be fed and the cows gathered in for milking while getting the little ones ready for school.

The older girls had to return to their boarding schools by mid-January (It was common practice for the children of the comfortably off farming class to be sent to boarding school). Indeed, it was probably just as well because she was forced to take up the reins of her life again. Gradually with the help of her brother Tom and two reliable farmhands, Joe and a young neighbouring lad called Billy, she was able to take over the management of the farm. This, alongside her care for the family, left her little time for brooding and indeed that was a blessing.

CHAPTER 7

Looking to her Family's Future

The children with their different characters were such a lively bunch that they brought interest and zest to her days, and gradually her joy in life returned. Dennis could always make her smile with his stories and droll accounts of people he met. For as long as she could remember he had been passionate about horses. She could recall watching him through the kitchen window when, only a little boy of seven or eight, he taught himself to ride their good-natured pony, bare-back. Again, and again he slipped off and Jenny would placidly continue to eat grass until he clambered back up. It was about a year before Pat died when, returning with Dennis from the point-to-point in Toomevara, the child had nearly toppled her in his excitement: "Mam, Mam, I'm going to be a jockey when I grow up." Little had she known then that he would become widely celebrated as someone who had a gift for training and healing horses, and that folk from throughout the county and beyond would make their way to Reiskmore to consult him. She recalled their neighbour, Pat Hogan who trained racehorses, watching him as a young boy as he took their old farm horse over the circle of fences he had erected on the lawn. "That boy has a real gift with horses Hanna," he told her, and indeed it was so.

Well, his love of horses, riding, and horsemanship did indeed become a lifelong passion, and one he shared with Jim. This created a strong bond between them. They both hunted with the North Tipperary foxhounds and each, at different times, became Master of Hounds. Both boys were regarded as good judges of horseflesh. Jim always maintained a racehorse on the farm and Dennis would be given the task of training this prized animal which he sometimes rode in local races. She smiled to recall his excitement on returning from Bruff point-to-point having unexpectedly ridden Jim's horse to victory.

"Well Mother dear, Fairie Pairc and myself tore strips off the competition today."

She had framed the photo of him that appeared in the paper. It was a proud day for them.

Jim too had been a fun-loving little boy but became quieter after his father died. Joe took him under his wing at that time, patiently including him in the work around the farm. Hanna believed that this laid the foundation of his interest in farming. He became very attached to Joe and she was thankful for it.

He must have been about eleven when Joe took him to his first fair in Nenagh. The single oil lamp cast glimmers of light on his tousled head when she roused him at five o'clock that morning. He seemed touchingly young to her as he excitedly pulled on his socks and boots. They made a hearty breakfast of bacon and eggs before setting out to drive the cattle the eight long miles into town. There, they met his uncle Tom who did the selling. She recalled the relish with which he regaled her with his new knowledge.

"You have to ask a lot more for the cattle than you think you'll get, Mam, and you pretend to let them wear you down, but you need to be sure that you don't go below what they're worth, and I got three bottles of lemonade and loads of biscuits," he added with a grin.

It must have been a year or so later when he returned from a fair in Borrisokane with his uncle Tom and told her proudly, "I sold nearly all the calves Mam."

"He's a natural Hanna," Tom added "I overheard him telling Micky Boyle, with not the glimmer of a smile, that his uncle would murder him if he sold them for any less, but that he'd split the difference, and sure Micky, God bless his innocence, thought he'd got a great bargain."

Jim would go on to be a very successful cattle dealer, buying not just for himself but for a number of the big Dublin dealers.

Joe had taken Dennis to the fairs too but, while he loved the banter and the stories told by the characters he met, he didn't take the same serious interest in the business of buying and selling that Jim did. When she'd enquired of Joe how he'd got on after one such fair, Joe was embarrassed and a little awkward.

"Well Missus I don't like to worry you but some of the lads at the fair think it great gas to give the young fellow a bottle of porter, and sometimes more than one, and bedad I'd be afraid he might take a liking for it."

This worried her, knowing his father's weakness for the drink.

Not long after this she had discussed the future paths of her boys with her brother Tom.

"Jim is clearly cut out for farming, Hanna, and maybe you should let him get started on managing it when he's finished the national school. He can always go to evening classes later to catch up."

She agreed and also accepted his suggestion that Dennis should be enrolled in Saint Flannan's school in Ennis.

"He's less steady than Jim," Tom told her, "and I'm not too happy about the amount of time he spends in the company of some of the local wild boys. The discipline of school life will turn his mind to more useful channels."

Dennis himself was quite happy with the proposal, feeling it to be a new adventure. She didn't know much about his life at school, though, years later heard that he was led into drink by some of the older boys. He loved returning to the farm for the summer holidays to pick up with old friends and he spent a lot of time with the horses. He would go quiet when he had to return to school but didn't complain.

Hanna sent Katie to the Brigidine convent school in Mount Rath which her Devaney cousin Stasia also attended. Following some discussion about Katie's experience in Mount Rath she was advised by Aunt Julia to send the girls to the Ursulines in Thurles.

"They prepare girls well for independent life, Hanna, and get very good results."

So it was that Bridie, Roisin and Eilin followed Mae and Peg to the Ursulines. This served them well as all her girls carved out successful lives for themselves. Eilin went into the civil service and Mae followed a career in hotel management while Roisin, having studied domestic science, became bean an ti (Gaelic for housekeeper) in the highly regarded Irish College in Ring Waterford. Hanna was proud of them and fondly recalled the fun and laughter that holiday periods brought to the old farmhouse. She also smiled to recall the relief, when all the noise and arguments were replaced by tranquillity on their departure.

CHAPTER 8

THE FAMILY SPREADS ITS WINGS

There was a lot of upheaval in the family around the summer of 1912-1913. Katie, her gentle eldest girl, spoke of what she believed to be her calling to the religious life. She admired the work of the Sisters of Mercy in Nenagh, particularly among the poor children of the town. This was the order to which she was drawn, and of which, in time, she was to become the Mother General. Hanna worried about her youth and Peg in particular was distressed at the thought of losing her best loved sister, but Katie remained firm in her determination to pursue her vocation.

The smell of floor polish would always call to mind that bleak parlour, with its picture of the crucified Christ gazing down from bare walls. There, Hanna said goodbye to her girl, both of them crying when the stern Mistress of Novices led her away. She had not anticipated the overwhelming wave of grief that swept over her as she tried to pray, "God's will be done." Katie was now lost to her, and her loneliness was intense. How she missed the comfort of her companionship. Katie had been a gentling presence in a family of such forceful personalities, soothing the abrasive conflicts that could sometimes arise.

There was little time for Hanna to indulge her grief as a painful challenge was to preoccupy her the following year.

This was not something she anticipated on receiving the joyful news that her youngest brother Willie was coming home for a holiday and looking forward to visiting her. Willie had been sent directly to New York following his ordination in Paris at the College des Irlandais, just a year prior to Pat's death. Handsome, clever and generous she was so proud of him and great was her delight on hearing of his proposed visit. How they enjoyed his marvellous tales of life in New York as he described to them his parish in Brooklyn. It was a late August afternoon during his visit and very hot. They were sipping homemade lemonade under the shade of the chestnut tree watching the young ones at tennis, and smiling at Dennis' irritation as Peg beat him yet again, when Willie broached the subject with her:

"It can't be easy for you raising this large brood on your own Hanna and I'd like to take one of them back with me, if you are willing. I could give them a good start in life."

She was taken aback and a little dismayed as the wound from the loss of Katie was still raw. Willie had been thinking about one of the boys but this was not feasible. Jim was to take over the farm and Dennis was adamant that he didn't want to go to New York. Tom was of course much too young to be considered. While she appreciated the advantages of such an offer for one of her girls it was with some anguish that she said,

"I will speak with Mae and Peg, but I'll leave it up to them Willie."

Peg was enthusiastic:

"I'd like to go Mam, sure I can always come home if I don't like it after a few years."

"That might cost a lot of money Peg," she responded dryly.

Though Mae as the eldest, had seemed the likely choice, she was reluctant to consider her uncle's offer, and it was soon settled that Peg would be the one. Willie discussed his proposal to send her to secretarial classes, expanding on the job opportunities that this would open up, and she was very excited by the new adventure that awaited her.

"God grant that this is the right decision for my girl and give me the strength to endure her loss," Hanna prayed nightly during this time. Then, with little time to spare before departure, preparations were frenetic and in no time there she was, standing on the platform of Nenagh railway station patting Peg's back as she clung to her, tears streaming down both of their faces.

Dennis put her cases in the train while Willie promised they'd write as soon as they arrived. Peg made her promise to write every week which indeed she did for a long number of years, something that helped to assuage the pain of her blithe girl's absence. How they looked forward to her letters crowded with strange images; markets overflowing with exotic fruits and vegetables, many of which they'd never heard of, olives, zucchini, egg plant, and peoples of all colours and creeds.

"We have lots of bearded men with ringleted hair that live near the Parish House. Maybe you'd like me to bring one of them back to Reiskmore?"

She wrote mischievously;

"But you can have your choice Mam, there are two fine strapping black men who work with Uncle Willie and loads of Chinese men looking for wives. You must let me know your wishes."

"Just you bring me back a nice Catholic Irishman" she'd replied firmly.

In the event Peg married Chris, a very wealthy friend of her uncle's. Chris was of German origin, and some eight years her senior. Over the following years it became clear that they lived the high life in New York. Her letters were full of parties, tennis tournaments, riding expeditions amongst the wealthy of the city. It all came to an end with the Great Wall Street crash when Chris lost all his money and sadly, it gradually emerged, sought solace in drink. Her poor girl. It was not difficult to read between the lines how difficult life became for her. The regret she felt then over her decision to let her go to New York had remained with her. Peg had to go out to work and, luckily, got a job as a counter assistant in Saks of Fifth Avenue.

They were awed by her description of this department store with its gilt framed mirrors, luxurious sofas for customers to rest upon and moving staircases, which Hanna didn't credit at first. It was only when Willie added a postscript to her following letter, "it's true Hanna they're called elevators," that she believed it. Indeed, she did not think that she would have been brave enough to step on one of those. Within a very short space of time, Peg was promoted and in fact became the chief buyer for women's fashions in this prestigious store and would remain the breadwinner of her household. Over the years ahead her sisters would benefit from her accounts of high fashion in New York and indeed, became remarkably fashionable and poised young women. Hanna recalled how it used to distress her youngest daughter, Eilin, that she would not agree to exchange her sober black garb for something brighter and more becoming.

She remembered praying for Peg during that time when it was the turn of Reiskmore to host the stations (The custom of celebrating Mass in the homes of parishioners). Hanna's house was shining, light sparkled on the clean windows and glinted off the lustre jug of daffodils on the kitchen table. Her best white linen tablecloth covered the sideboard in the dining-room which had been arranged as an altar. Two little posies of primroses gathered from the fields were placed alongside the candlesticks on either side of the makeshift tabernacle. The family and some of the neighbours knelt in hushed silence as Father Hogan began Mass. How deeply she felt the aura of sacredness that enveloped them all then, as she did whenever the sacred mysteries were celebrated in her home. It was Tom who served at the Mass and she remembered being struck by the beauty of the child with his dark glossy hair, almost too regular features and velvet brown eyes. She recalled the premonition she had on that occasion that he was destined for the priesthood, though he would surely have broken hearts had he decided otherwise.

Some months later he went fishing with his uncle Tom and returned in high good humour with two good sized trout.

"They looked golden brown in the water Mam but then turned sort of speckled when we knocked them on the head," and he smiled rather shyly at her.

When he left the room Tom told her that he'd talked to him about becoming a missionary priest.

"I did try to turn his thoughts to the Diocesan needs," he told her wryly, "but he seems to have his heart set on a missionary order and mentioned the Redemptorists."

"I imagine that's because he was very taken with the young Redemptorist who visited their school last autumn on returning from India," she replied.

When Tom persisted in this wish she made arrangements for him to attend the Redemptorist Juniorate in Limerick, considering it a great blessing on the family to have a son a priest and thanked God for it. Truth to tell, she was not sorry to see him safely settled at school as political turmoil began to spread throughout a country which was becoming increasingly dangerous, particularly for young men.

CHAPTER 9

IRELAND'S STRUGGLE COMES CALLING

It was 1914 when she realised that Jim and Dennis were keen to join the national struggle. They were influenced by her brother Rody Cleary and their cousins Jim and Tom Devaney all of whom were committed to the cause. The Devaney boys were close in age to her sons and had already joined the Irish National Volunteers.

"It will be good for the boys to join," Rody urged her, "give them healthy exercise and discipline. Besides," he added, "we need to mobilise to counteract the threat posed by the Ulster Unionists who have secured arms with the help of the Brits, and by God haven't the army officers up in the curragh asserted that they'd resign rather than move against Ulster Unionists."

Rumours of gun running for the Volunteers were rife around then. She read in the *Nenagh News* that the crown forces had fired on an innocent crowd in Dublin, killing four, because they failed to find a pile of guns imported by the nationalists. She recalled Rody's rage:

"Shot down like dogs, though God knows they'd turned a blind eye to the Ulster Unionists when they recruited firearms.

There will be civil war over this Hanna, one law for the Prods and another for the Catholics."

Hanna had been aware of the growing unease in the country during the previous years, though indeed she was preoccupied at the time with the foot and mouth crisis then spreading amongst the local farms. Then, there was all the excitement generated by the passing of the Home Rule Bill in May 1914. Jim was jubilant on returning from Nenagh where he and his cousins joined the celebrations.

"Oh Mam it was grand. There were hundreds of Volunteers marching and tar barrels flaming in the streets. The bands were playing *A Nation Once Again*. You should have seen all the people and there were bonfires lighting up the hills around the town."

She recalled being pleased, hoping that this was the end of the fighting. How wrong she had been. She didn't know whether to be glad or sorry when the Great War broke out shortly after and John Redmond urged the volunteers to fight for Britain, which had greatly reduced their ranks. She was certainly glad that neither of her boys got caught up in this awful war. Little did she know then, that one of the boy's heroes at that time, Frank McGrath, was also a member of the hard line IRB (Irish Republican Brotherhood). It was hard not to like Frank who was a great GAA man (Gaelic Athletic Association) and a terrific hurler, playing for the Toomevara Greyhounds. Tom Devaney and "Widger" Meagher, another Volunteer admired by the boys, also played for the Toomevara senior team. Frank McGrath, together with a small core of Volunteers who refused to fight for Britain, was responsible for building up the Irish Volunteers during this period. He used his links with the GAA to recruit local young men, amongst them Jim and Dennis. They, like all their friends, were mad about hurling. The GAA, Sinn Fein and the Volunteers were all hand in glove around Toomevara, so it was inevitable that her boys would become caught up in the impending conflict. How she prayed to keep them from harm and, indeed, in the beginning it was nothing more than drilling and exercising.

Jim was ravenously hungry when he returned from the Nenagh fair on Easter Monday 1916. "I got good prices for our yearlings Mam," he said between mouthfuls "but something strange happened because the four o'clock train to Dublin was stopped and I heard that all the trains to Dublin were stopped."

It was a week or so later that the Nenagh Guardian announced that Sinn Feiners had taken a portion of the city, but nobody seemed to know the full story and there was a lot of confusion. Many folk thought that it was some young hotheads and hoped things would calm down. She had laughed when she heard that, at a meeting of the Nenagh Board of Guardians, somebody asserted that the suffragettes were at the root of it. Soon, however, news of the executions of the leaders trickled through and she, alongside most of the neighbours became indignant. "They were fine God-fearing young men most of them, Hanna," Mary Anne said when she visited that week. Indeed, Hanna had never forgotten the beautiful lines from a poem by one of them, Joseph Plunkett:

I see his blood upon the rose
And in the stars the glory of his eyes
His body gleams amid eternal snows
His tears fall from the skies.

CHAPTER 10

Personal Anguish amid the Struggle

In September 1917 they were again shocked on hearing of the death of Thomas Ashe who had been a founding member of the Irish Volunteers. In prison, and weakened by hunger strike, his death was caused by the brutality of force-feeding. It was after this that Jim told her, "We've been instructed to drill in public," and her anxiety increased. Frank McGrath was arrested for his part in this public drilling. He was released a couple of months later and the boys were amongst the huge crowd gathered in Nenagh to welcome him back. Hanna was startled to hear of so many peaceable law-abiding folk becoming ardent Republicans, and when it looked like the authorities might enforce conscription it seemed as if all the young men in the county had joined the Volunteers in protest, though indeed many of them fell away when the fear of this subsided.

She knew that a lot of men, particularly from Nenagh, had enlisted in the British war effort. Her cousin Mary Bergin who lived in the town spoke of the rising rate of crime among the young.

"There are no fathers, or any men left in the families to keep them in order Hanna," she told her.

"You need to keep away from those young hooligans that gather to fight at the market cross," she warned Dennis who was more inclined to meet his friends in the town.

Hanna smiled at a happier memory from that time when Mary Anne and Ellie insisted that the three of them should wrap up well and take the trap to Dromineer - it must have been during that bitter spell sometime in January 1917. They heard that the lake was frozen over. "I wonder if it's true Hanna?" They couldn't believe it, but indeed it was, and they were enthralled. The frozen lake, silvered under a wintry sun, was encircled by an army of icicled reeds against a background of glittering trees and hedges. They watched their boys skating on the ice-locked water, some of them even hurling. It was a magical afternoon in spite of the bitter cold.

The following year a much darker event was seared into her memory. This was when her youngest son Jack, a lively twelve-year old, died. It began, she recalled, with Tom and Jack complaining of sore throats. They had lost their usual high spirits and become listless and fretful. It was when Jack began to have difficulty swallowing that she became seriously alarmed and sent for the doctor. He could see the swelling on his throat with the tell-tale white spots and diagnosed diphtheria. During the days that followed they nursed both boys, applying the recommended solution of glycerine, hyposulphite and water directly to their throats.

"Oh, Mam, Jack can't even swallow a tiny drop of water."

Mae came downstairs, tears pouring down her face. Hanna held him in her arms while he slipped into a coma and died some hours later. It was Mae who came and took his young body from her and she watched dazed as the girls washed and laid him out in his confirmation suit. She would recall the physical pain it cost her to wrench her mind from the image of that frail corpse to focus on keeping Tom, still very weak and unaware of his brother's death, alive.

"Make up a bed for him in my bedroom," she told Mae.

"Oh Lord, have pity and do not take him from me too," she prayed in desperation.

Thankfully Tom gradually recovered. When they laid Jack's body beside Pat's in Ballygibbon graveyard, she knew that a part of her remained buried there too.

It was hard for Hanna to share her brother Rody's enthusiasm for the McDonagh club, founded in Nenagh around this time.

"We now have our own Sinn Fein club, and by God I think I'll join."

He was surely elated by the general election results at the end of 1918.

"We've swept the boards all over the country and the old Irish Parliamentary Party is gone, 'tis the Sinn Fein Republicans who now speak for Nationalist Ireland."

Among them for North Tipperary was Joe McDonagh though, like his fellow Sinn Fein MPs, he refused to take his seat in Westminster and was still in Reading gaol. Hanna recalled how useful the local Sinn Fein club was in the winter of 1917/1918, organising food distribution amongst the poor in Nenagh. Because of the war, they were hard hit by the escalating food prices and the appalling weather conditions that winter. Indeed, the poor folk of Nenagh would have faced famine conditions had it not been for the sterling work of the Vincent de Paul Society. She was very aware of how fortunate they, and other farmers were, in benefiting from the increased prices for their cattle, butter and eggs which the war afforded. And she was glad to join them in donating a good quantity of potatoes to the relief effort.

In the summer of 1918 an outbreak of the dreaded Spanish Influenza took the lives of some thirty people in Nenagh before it abated in early 1919, but thankfully the family wasn't affected. She had hoped that the worst was then behind them, and had little expected the turmoil that was to engulf both her family and country over the years to follow.

CHAPTER 11

A Truce is Declared and a Treaty Signed

The opening shots of the Irish War of Independence were fired in South Tipperary in January 1919. This occurred just a couple of hours before Dail Eireann met formally for the first time. Rather than take their seats at Westminster the newly elected Sinn Fein Representatives constituted themselves as 'Dail Eireann' (the assembly of Ireland) in Dublin, adopting a declaration of independence and a constitution.

Two policemen were shot during an ambush at Soloheadbeg in South Tipperary and it wasn't long before two more policemen were killed during the rescue of prisoners. The Devaney cousins and Jim were in the house and she recalled her anger at their excited chatter.

"It's not a game boys and that's four families mourning the loss of their sons, the Lord have mercy on them. Was it really necessary to kill the poor men who were only doing their jobs."

"It's war Aunt Hanna," Tom Devaney replied, "and the police are fighting for Britain."

"We've sworn allegiance to the Dail Mam so now we're the Irish Republican Army," Jim told her in August 1919.

Well, the war came even closer that summer when the RIC Inspector Michael Hunt was shot going home from Thurles races and another officer Phil Brady was shot near Lorrha in September. They were local men, known to them, and Hanna was troubled.

During these fraught years all meetings including fairs and markets were banned. Between the banning of these and the disruption of railway services, they had the additional worry of trying to get their cattle and produce sold. She was highly indignant when a young policeman stopped her on her way into Nenagh in the spring of 1920:

"You need to get down Missus and empty your bag and Constable O'Brien will search the cart."

"I can tell you I have more to do than be play-acting with guns," she said crossly.

"Orders is Orders Missus, get down please."

Indeed, from then on, road blocks and searchings' became frequent occurrences on entering or leaving the town.

The RIC as well as the military were now officially the enemy and she could see that attitudes were hardening on both sides. It was in March 1920 when two young policemen were shot in Toomevara that she became increasingly fearful for her boys. She knew that they were out with their comrades on raids and ambushes and burning police barracks. Like the other young men Jim and Dennis were now fully armed. They were very quiet on returning home one evening in the spring of 1920 and Jim looked very shaken.

"We burnt down Ballymackey barracks," he said, when she asked what had happened. Jim had always got on well with the sergeant and was distressed.

"We had to Mam but I explained to his missus that we were required to do it and that she could take her time getting out as much of her stuff as possible."

Hanna's home was a known safe house for gunmen on the run and because of this they were subject to sporadic raids by the police and military. It was common for both her boys to sleep away from home in other safe houses or barns during this time to avoid the raids, and for other young men to use their house as a safe haven when their own homes were being searched.

"For the Lord's sake boys, don't leave your guns thrown on the stairs, you may as well hand them in if you're going to be so careless," she said crossly one Saturday afternoon when four of them arrived starving.

They had been on the run for two days. She got out a sheet made of old flour bags and had just wrapped the guns loosely in it, and buried them under the meal in the big wooden chest in the scullery, when young Kitty Hall arrived. She was breathless and told them that there were two military lorries coming their way. The boys cut out through the haggard and hid in the lower fields while Kitty and herself whipped out some old socks that needed darning and were sitting peaceably by the fire when they arrived. Thankfully they didn't search the meal chest.

Hanna was surprised to hear that people spoke well of the arbitration courts set up by Sinn Fein in opposition to the

Crown courts, and that many people were now using them to settle disputes. However, the round of shootings and reprisals continued and there was a lot of disquiet because tension had arisen among the leaders. This led to a botched attempt on Borrisokane barracks and the death of one of their local Volunteers, Michael Kennedy. Then there was the shooting and wounding of a policeman as a reprisal for Terence McSwiney's death (Terence MacSwiney, Mayor of Cork, died in prison while on hunger strike) leading to yet more military raids. Flannery's shop in Nenagh was burnt down. The Flannery's were good friends and she was saddened to hear of their fate.

"Captain Hambleton threatened to kill Father O'Halloran." Mary Anne told her on returning from Nenagh a couple of days later and this was truly shocking. Indeed, it was no surprise to hear that Captain Hambleton, in turn, was shot the following night. She couldn't recall whether it was then or earlier that they'd heard of the Black and Tan's raid on the Bishop's palace in Ennis in an assassination attempt. Doctor Michael Fogarty, Bishop of Killaloe was her cousin and an outspoken supporter of the fight for independence. Hanna was grateful that he was safely away in Dublin at the time.

Towards the end of 1920 her brother Rody, who was a Sinn Fein councillor, arrived in Reiskmore very early.

"Hanna where are the boys?" He asked urgently.

"They're rounding up the milkers, what's wrong Rody, what is it?" she replied anxiously.

"They need to get away to a safe place, the military are on the rampage, they firebombed loads of buildings including the creamery and raided my house last night," he told her. "The two young O'Briens had come out of the town for safety and were staying with us and didn't they bayonet and shoot them, the blackguards. Those boys were not even active members of the IRA."

She watched with heightened anxiety as the raids and shootings continued. Then in December 1920 Martial Law was proclaimed which meant that there were no fairs or markets. In addition there had been no rail travel out of the town since the rail strike the previous May, and all this, together with the burning of the creamery meant that they, along with the other farmers, were badly hit yet again. Trading either livestock or produce became very difficult.

She never forgot that morning towards the end of January 1921. It was bitterly cold and she recalled the icy feel of the handle as she pumped water for the house outside the back door. Jim was already in the yard shovelling manure onto a cart when Dennis cycled in, going immediately to talk to his brother. It was only an hour since he had set out for Con Spain's in Kilruane to treat a sick foal and she hadn't expected him back so soon. Both of them turned to her and she knew from the stricken look on their faces that something terrible had happened.

"Jim Devaney was shot," Jim said baldly.

"He's only twenty one, he'll recover" she replied foolishly.

"He's dead Mam he's not going to recover."

She could hardly believe it. That young man so full of life, and so familiar to her, dead.

Then the news emerged over the following days that he hadn't died of the wound but from loss of blood and exposure.

"His comrades fled Mam, making their own way home and taking his gun with them," Jim told her. "He was in O'Meara's pub in Kilruane with three other volunteers when the police came along in a Crossley tender and spotted one of them running into the shed where the others were. They tried to make a break for it but were chased by the police, both lots firing at each other."

The police had then gone off to get reinforcements and came back to search the area, finding Jim's body in the ditch.

"Some comrades, to leave him like that and concentrate on saving their own cowardly skins. By God they should be court martialled."

The boys and indeed the neighbours were angered by this and by the failure of local people to go to his aid. The anxiety escalated still further during those first months of 1921 when four members of the volunteers were killed and it was rumoured that there were leaks within the active service unit as well as some problem drinking amongst the leaders. She could see how demoralising this was for the boys and their comrades.

Hanna could hardly believe it when, around this same time, Dennis rushed in, en route for another safe house to tell her, "Mam, the Black and Tans have forced Uncle Rody to travel with them as a hostage when they go out on raids. They're making Volunteer officers or Sinn Fein officials travel in front of the lorries with them for protection."

Would it never end? She had frequent nightmares in which Dennis or Jim, and sometimes both of them were nailed to the front of the Black and Tan lorries with their comrades taking pot shots at them. It was truly a nightmarish time.

It was only a few weeks after his brother Jim's death that Tom Devaney was also shot. Tom had been visiting his parents farm in Pallas when the police and Auxiliaries raided. (The Auxiliaries were veteran British army officers sent over to assist the RIC). One of them spotted a man running away. They gave chase and shot Tom in the back claiming that he refused to halt when they called, though a witness claimed they never called halt.

It had surely been a scene of desolation that greeted Hanna's arrival for the wake.

"Oh Mary Anne, I am so sorry."

"Sure we all knew it might happen Hanna but it's hard, it's hard. God and his Blessed mother give me strength. How could he take my two boys, oh, how could he take my two boys?"

His father, Michael Devaney, watched them shoot a second son and never recovered. He too was dead by the end of December 1922. Three deaths in the family within two years, the Lord have mercy on their souls. It was no surprise that Mary Anne was never the same after that.

Hanna's anxiety for her boys was at fever pitch and when Sean O Leary was shot in Moneygall on Good Friday 1921, and his comrade Eddie John Ryan cruelly tortured by the Black and Tans, she prayed ceaselessly for this terrible conflict to end. There was a final ambush near Cloughjordan in June 1921 and then in July, her prayers were answered and a Truce was declared. How relieved they all were when the Treaty was formally signed in December 1921 and all prisoners and internees were released. In January 1922 the provisional Irish government headed by Michael Collins became the first government of the Irish Free State.

In spite of all the tragedy it was a proud day for the country. Hanna would always remember the 14th February 1922, when she stood beside her sons in Nenagh to watch the military evacuating the barracks and a company of fully equipped IRA men take possession and raise the Republican flag. That night hundreds of people from the countryside joined in the celebrations. Young folk stayed in town to watch the RIC evacuate the police barracks next day and cheer our own Republican police who moved into Kenyon Street barracks. She went home thankful and relieved and, though tired out, got down on her knees and offered up a rosary of thanksgiving that the conflict was over.

CHAPTER 12

THE HORROR OF CIVIL WAR

By the time the Truce arrived, the Rural District and Urban Councils were in the hands of Sinn Fein. They had established their own law courts, and these were already functioning. It was good to see the fairs and markets return and the restrictions on cyclists and motorists lifted. However, all Volunteer activity did not cease, as required by the conditions of the Truce. Hanna saw a party of fifteen or twenty IRA men parading in full uniform when she visited a shop in Cloughjordan, which purchased her eggs, and for a long time you'd see groups of them standing around in the local towns seeming to proclaim victory. IRA training camps continued and anniversaries or burials were marked by a formal display of Volunteers in full uniform and with gun salutes.

Cumann na mBan, too, continued to fundraise for the cause. This was the woman's branch of Sinn Fein which had been very active throughout the Troubles and Mae, Bridie and latterly Roisin were involved. They had loved the fundraising activities, organising dances, concerts and levies and having fun with other young people. Indeed, they had also acted as couriers delivering warnings to the Volunteers. They were particularly valuable as messengers because of being able to move around with ease, as the authorities didn't believe that such young girls would be directly involved in the struggle.

Hanna was always anxious when they were out on such missions.

It must have been in August or September of 1921 that she overheard Bridie and Roisin planning to meet their friends at a levy. She put her foot down:

"No Bridie, I'll not have you and Roisin standing outside the church on Sunday collecting, it breaks the conditions of the Truce and just gives the police an excuse to restart the violence".

She had already heard of a police assault on an IRA man in Newport and she didn't want to give them another excuse. As the spring rolled into the summer of 1922 they watched with trepidation as some local hardliners continued to burn or damage the property of the Anglo-Irish families, who were very vulnerable. She recalled that Ballygibbon house, the rectory at Ballinaclough, and Lord Dunalley's home all suffered such attacks. Worse still, was the terrible outrage done to a young protestant woman in Dromineer by four local IRA volunteers. She was ashamed of her countrymen then and had heard that the poor young woman fled to England and never returned.

Hanna was aware of the escalating bitterness and fighting between the Pro-Treaty and Anti-Treaty factions. Like many of her neighbours she watched with horror as the country once again slid into conflict with many of the hard-line Republican Volunteers wanting to fight on, and refusing to accept the ongoing requirement of an oath of allegiance to the Crown. She and her neighbours were happy to accept Michael Collins' recommendation to abide by the Treaty as the best deal that could be negotiated. Indeed, they could never have imagined achieving so much even a decade ago. Thankfully most North Tipperary councils voted also to accept.

"I would be heart-broken", she told Jim and Dennis, "if either of you were to be drawn into this fight which will end with Irishmen killing each other".

"Lord, you needn't worry Mam," I can guarantee you that I'm never, ever, going to sleep in a hay shed again", Dennis said.

She laughed because she knew how tormented both boys had been by insect bites while on the run. However, she also knew that after their cousins' deaths and the experience of divisions among their leaders and some dubious conduct on the part of others, that their zest for the fight had waned. In addition, they were tired of a way of life that had taken its toll, not only in terms of lives, but also in terms of their own high ideals.

The fighting seemed to take place mostly in South Tipperary, Limerick and further south, though she did recall one occasion when an old comrade of Jim's, then fighting on the Anti-Treaty side, sought shelter and food while on the run, and the boys helped him escape but otherwise, were not drawn into the conflict.

"I'm not going to shoot the men I slept with," Jim assured her.

It was hard to hear of some of his former comrades being executed by fellow-Irishmen, but she appreciated that it had to be ended, "and thanks be to God it was".

It was astonishing to learn that Pat's nephew, Norman Loughnane, had come over from London as secretary to the British Viceroy for the Treaty negotiations in Dublin. Norman was high up in the British civil service, but she knew that he had also been active in supporting the Irish Home Rule and Land Reform movement when younger, which made him seem a surprising choice. He wasn't in contact with them over the years of the fight for independence, fearing, as he explained later, that this would compromise them. He told them that the British officials were not keen on him for the post, but that the Irish delegates and particularly Tim Healy, who was involved with the Irish Parliamentary Party for years and was a seasoned parliamentarian, had pressed for his inclusion. Healy would later become the first Governor of the Irish Free State.

The death of Michael Collins at the hands of the Anti-Treaty forces in August 1922, just when the civil war was dying down and the forces of the Free State had re-established control, shocked the entire country. Doctor Fogarty who had celebrated the Requiem Mass in Dublin gave them details of the ambush on a visit soon after.

"It was truly heart wrenching Hanna, after all he'd been through and just months before he was due to marry Kitty (Kitty Kiernan and Michael Collins were due to be married in November 1922), God rest his brave soul".

He was almost in tears as indeed were they all. Michael Collins had been their hero and loyalty to his memory would make it difficult for them to forgive Eamonn De Valera for his part in promoting the Anti-Treaty movement. This, thankfully, was the final anguish of those troubled times to visit the family.

CHAPTER 13

A Return to Calmer Waters

How the years had whizzed by, and how strange that periods of contentment should be so much less memorable than those fraught with anxiety. Husbands and grandchildren arrived in quick succession. It was good to see Bridie's contentment following her marriage to a local farmer; she was so stricken when an earlier engagement to an Army Officer ended on his death. Mae, too, weathered a broken engagement and moved on, to a successful career in hotel management, while Roisin's humorous warm-hearted husband Alf Wrixon, a dentist, was a favourite with everyone. Eileen's husband Tom Donovan, a distinguished Dublin barrister was someone whose profound faith and integrity she admired. For herself, it was a surprise to discover that, while she loved to see her grandchildren, she was also glad when they left and her peaceful home was restored to her. She found it difficult to remember all their names!

Of course, Hanna's life became easier with modern conveniences. How fearful she was of the motor car at first: she worried that it might not stop quickly enough, it seemed so out of control. She was glad of its comfort now, welcoming the protection from wind and rain especially in winter.

"Well Mam you can have the first bath."

The new internal bathroom was finished and she and the boys admired the brand new bath standing on its chubby little legs with hot and cold water on tap. Gone was the wearisome task of carrying heavy buckets of water in from the pump to heat over the fire. Best of all was the toilet with its own tank of water and chain to flush it clean. How fresh the upstairs bedrooms became with no chamber pots lurking under beds.

She laughed aloud to recall the arrival of the wireless. She could still picture Joe's face when he came into the kitchen for his dinner. He stared at the set which was relaying the news, his face turning white under his tan, and started backing out of the room pointing at the set, "Jesus, Mary and Joseph help us, there's a divil in that box Ma'am!"

Hanna's main companions over the years since those troubled times were her sons, Jim and Dennis. They provided restful companionship, preoccupied as they were with their own interests. Many was the evening when they would sit with her and play cards, forty five or poker. Sometimes a neighbour or friend would drop by and join in the game, and they would chat until she served up tea and cake for supper. Jim always insisted that they play for money as he loved the excitement of a gamble. Often on a Sunday afternoon she would light the fire in the parlour and they would gather around the piano singing some of the old songs under the startled gaze of the stuffed pheasant that sat atop the instrument.

"Let you play us a waltz Jim."

Dennis would say, and, ignoring her protests, whirl her up into a dance around the small parlour, miraculously avoiding any damage. However, it was their willingness to kneel down with her to say the rosary every night before going to bed that gave her most comfort.

It was lovely, too, to watch all the young people having fun together when the girls visited with their husbands and wee ones.

"I'll put up the net and mark out the lawn," Jim, who was very keen on tennis, would say. And what lovely images remained with her. The girls so lithe and fresh and the young men full of banter and very competitive, no doubt to impress the girls.

Friends and neighbours would often drop in and she could recall several girls who were, no doubt, very aware of her two eligible sons. It was a little sad now to remember how popular Dennis was and how many attractive girls flocked around him. She thought that he might settle down with a wonderful horsewoman whom he courted for a long time. She could hardly recall her name now, her memory was not what it used to be. She did remember that the relationship ended with her marrying a great friend of Jim's. She didn't know how Dennis felt, maybe he was relieved, he might have found the responsibility oppressive.

Hanna worried about Jim's love for horse-racing, fearing that he gambled more than was wise. She was glad when, on returning from Lisdoonvarna, he told her that he had met the girl he hoped to marry. She felt that this would be a steadying influence. Nevertheless, it was with mixed feelings that she welcomed Mabel Corbett to her home.

She was a charming and polished young woman who would inherit a half of her father's substantial farm. She had already made it clear to Jim that she wanted them to have their own home, and explained to Hanna that her own mother or father would come to live with her, whenever one of them passed away. Indeed, truth to tell, she was relieved. She had been her own mistress for too long to easily relinquish control of the household and she sensed that Mabel too was a strong-minded woman and indeed it was for the best that they each had their own households. Hanna's own girls were disappointed, having hoped that Jim's marriage would secure her care in her old age, but God was Good and she wasn't worried about that.

It was hard on Dennis who relied, probably more than he realised, on his brother's companionship. He had always enjoyed a drink but now began to go to the pub more frequently and, while she knew it assuaged his loneliness, she did worry about the hold alcohol was taking on his life. It was one of her biggest crosses to watch this blithe talented son of hers losing any sense of direction over the years.

There had been a number of projects, none of which came to anything, such as plans for a riding school with a neighbouring enthusiast. Jim offered to help with the purchase of a local farm that came on the market, but Dennis didn't want the responsibility. He had always been a great reader and was particularly attracted to literature about the settling of the west in America. He believed that his talent and skills in horsemanship would be useful there and he got as far as making all arrangements for emigrating. Though, sad at the thought of losing this well-loved son, Hanna had encouraged him. It was not to be.

"I couldn't do it Mam," he said, returning from the station on the day scheduled for his departure.

Of course, anything to do with horses always aroused his interest.

"Good morning Mrs Loughnane, is Dinny around."

It was the beginning of their young neighbour's summer holidays. Piers Skidmore was home from his boarding school in England and his first port of call was Dennis who taught him to ride and handle horses. The Skidmore land bordered theirs and for a time he would cross the Ollatrim river every day to put the lad through his paces. Dennis took pride in Piers' horsemanship as he became proficient in hunting and showing at Nenagh's annual show, and nurtured hopes of conquests at the Dublin horse show but this was not to be.

Hanna overheard him say to Jim,

"You know we should put Piers up to ride On the Tiles, (Jim's recently purchased thoroughbred), "in the local point to point."

He was sorely disappointed when Piers' family vetoed this proposal. Their friendship, however, remained solid and it mattered little to either that one was Protestant and the other Catholic

It was a comfort to Hanna that both her boys cherished friendships across the Irish/Anglo-Irish divide which was healing for both communities. Piers told her how much they enjoyed the tales with which Dennis would regale them after Mass on Sunday when he would join the family for a glass of sherry. This became a ritual that they all looked forward to. Indeed, he was a great story-teller just like his father, God rest his soul. She had accepted by then that he would be with her, and however distressed she was by his drinking she was grateful for his companionship over these last years.

But above all it was the depth of his faith that gave Hanna most hope for a safe future for him. She smiled to recall a neighbour's astonishment on one occasion when his friend Father McGrath called to collect him to take him to Lough Derg, where both were to undertake the arduous three-day pilgrimage.

"You're going to fast for three days and walk around that stony place on your bare feet and stay up all night? You must be mad Dinny."

"Yes Mikey, but don't tell anyone, t'would ruin my good name," Dennis replied, leaving Mikey aghast!

Indeed, Mikey didn't know, nor did many folk, that this was something that Dennis undertook every year. She had no doubt that God would forgive him his weakness for the drink.

Her own faith had been the bedrock of her life. She was at peace now, confident that this faith would continue to infuse the lives of her family.

Epilogue

Johanna Loughnane died of a heart attack at the age of eighty one during the Easter weekend of April 1955.

Revisiting Reiskmore in recent years, as the old homestead crumbles away, has been an exercise in elegiac rumination. I cannot open the latch gate that leads to the front door, its rusting framework imprisoned in a dense tangle of thorny bushes. Gone are the well-kept flower beds and freshly painted railings that enclosed its once attractive frontage, while the solid old farmhouse is imploding inwards with the collapse of its roof. The farmyard, and outhouses too, are displaying all the signs of decay and neglect, though still partially in use by neighbouring farmers. It is hard to conceive of the passionate and energetic lives once enfolded by those sturdy sheltering walls.

I am conscious too of the disappearance of a way of life familiar to Hanna and to the farming community all over Ireland, its joys and hardships replaced by different, though doubtless no less challenging issues. Gone, too, is the comfort of the old certainties enshrined in the religious beliefs and convictions that governed the minutiae of their lives. Hanna belonged to a strong farming class heavily invested in the structure and authority of the church, the ranks of its religious orders and priesthood peopled by the sons and daughters of this sector of Irish society. The shocking abuses perpetrated by so many priests and those in religious orders would have been unimaginable to Hanna, and indeed, to her sons and daughters. I imagine it would have been painful for them to confront the sufferings meted out to those who fell victim to a cruel and rigid imposition of the church's harsh judgements. The disgrace visited on the church over recent decades has left its authority threadbare and it has been good to see a more open, compassionate society begin to emerge.

As someone who benefited from the decency, care and sense of service also instilled by that same faith, I hope that a Christian church informed by the urge to serve rather than judge will continue to support my fellow countrymen and women.

Reading List

Joseph Lee, The *Modernisation of Irish Society*, 1848 to 1918, Gill & McMillan, 1973.
Joseph Lee, *Ireland, 1912 to 1985*, Cambridge University Press, 1989.
David Hogan (pseudonym for Frank Gallagher),*The Four Glorious Years*, Irish Press Ltd, 1953.
Joe Ambrose, *Sean Tracey and the Tan War*, Mercier Press, 2007.
Dan Breen, *My Fight for Freedom*, Anvil books, 1924.
Eunan O'Halpin & Daithi O'Corrain, *The Dead of the Irish Revolution*, Yale University Press, 2020.
Richard Killeen, *Timeline of Irish History*, Gill & Macmillan, 2003.
Kevin M Griffin & Kevin A Griffin, The *Renihan Diaries*, Ballina Killaloe Print, 2005.
Kevin Danaher, *In Ireland Long Ago*, Mercier Press, 1964.
Eoin Swithin Walsh, Kilkenny, *In Times of Revolution 1900-1923*, Merrion Press, 2018.
R F Foster, *Vivid Faces: The Revolutionary Generation in Ireland 1890-1923*, Allen Lane, 2014.
Gerard Dooley, *Nenagh, 1914-21; Years of Crisis*, Four Courts Press, 2015.
Sean Hogan, *The Black and Tans in North Tipperary; Policing Revolution and War 1913-1922*, Nenagh Guardian publications, 2013.
Harry Howard, And the *Harvest is done: Life on the Land in Offaly and Tipperary*, Geography Publications, 1990.

Patrick Devaney, (brother of Jim and Tom Devaney), *The Devaney Families*, hand-written account, 1996.

Peirs Skidmore, *Dennis Loughnane , A personal reminiscence.*

Con Spain, *The Dark Days of 1921 remembered,* The Cloughjordan Heritage, Vol. 4, 1996.

Web sites used https://www.historyireland.com

Acknowledgements

I owe a debt of gratitude to the many friends, family members and kindly strangers who took an interest in this project and helped to bring it to fruition. My sisters Marie, Kathleen, Mairead, Gemma and brother Jim, as well as my cousins Maire Donovan, Carmel and Joan Grace, Michael Harty and Orla Cleary all helped with information about the family history. Marie in particular went to the trouble of liaising with various members of the family to establish as much clarity as possible, thank you Marie. I am also indebted to the historical sources which are outlined in the reading list. I owe particular thanks to the authors of two excellent local histories dealing with the area during the period with which the story is concerned: Sean Hogan's *The Black and Tans in North Tipperary* and Gerard Dooley's *Nenagh, 1914-1921, Years of Crisis*.

My daughter-in-law, Laura Donnelly, a talented graphic designer based in the Scottish Borders, is responsible for the cover design, which incorporates images of my grandmother, and uncle Dennis as well as the Reiskmore homestead in happier days. Many thanks Laura.

I need to thank my friends, Peter O'Beirne, Moya Cannon, Maureen Kinnell and Katherine Dickie, who generously read through my early drafts and provided helpful feedback. This was supplemented by the rigorous editorial scrutiny of my husband Jim, daughters Orna and Maeve and friend

Christine Hoy. I want to add a particular thank you to Sean Hogan (mentioned above) for his generosity in correcting a number of errors and providing excellent advice. All the above have helped to make the final product a leaner more readable document; thank you all. Additional thanks to Katherine for helping devise a simplified family tree.

Finally I need to thank Jim for his unfailing support and encouragement in this, as in all other areas of my life.

Lightning Source UK Ltd.
Milton Keynes UK
UKHW010725171121
394120UK00001B/111